How To Use This Study Guide

This five-lesson study guide corresponds to *"The Tragic Mistake of Moral Surrender" With Rick Renner* (Renner TV). Each lesson in this study guide covers a topic that is addressed during the program series, with questions and references supplied to draw you deeper into your own private study of the Scriptures on this subject.

To derive the most benefit from this study guide, consider the following:

First, watch or listen to the program prior to working through the corresponding lesson in this guide. (Programs can also be viewed at **renner.org** by clicking on the Media/Archive links or on our Renner Ministries YouTube channel.)

Second, take the time to look up the scriptures included in each lesson. Prayerfully consider their application to your own life.

Third, use a journal or notebook to make note of your answers to each lesson's Study Questions and Practical Application challenges.

Fourth, invest specific time in prayer and in the Word of God to consult with the Holy Spirit. Write down the scriptures or insights He reveals to you.

Finally, take action! Whatever the Lord tells you to do according to His Word, do it.

For added insights on this subject, it is recommended that you obtain Rick Renner's book *Last Days Survival Guide*. You may also select from Rick's other available resources by placing your order at **renner.org** or by calling 1-800-742-5593.

LESSON 1

TOPIC

The Tragic Mistake of Moral Surrender

SCRIPTURES

1. **Genesis 2:7-9** — And the Lord God formed man of the dust of the ground, and breathed into his nostrils the breath of life; and man became a living soul. And the Lord God planted a garden eastward in Eden; and there he put the man whom he had formed. And out of the ground made the Lord God to grow every tree that is pleasant to the sight, and good for food; the tree of life also in the midst of the garden, and the tree of knowledge of good and evil.

2. **Genesis 2:15** — And the Lord God took the man, and put him into the garden of Eden to dress it and to keep it.

3. **Genesis 2:16,17** — And the Lord God commanded the man, saying, Of every tree of the garden thou mayest freely eat: But of the tree of the knowledge of good and evil, thou shalt not eat of it: for in the day that thou eatest thereof thou shalt surely die.

4. **Genesis 2:18-20** — And the Lord God said, It is not good that the man should be alone; I will make him an help meet for him. And out of the ground the Lord God formed every beast of the field, and every fowl of the air; and brought them unto Adam to see what he would call them: and whatsoever Adam called every living creature, that was the name thereof. And Adam gave names to all cattle, and to the fowl of the air, and to every beast of the field; but for Adam there was not found an help meet for him.

5. **Genesis 2:21,22** — And the Lord God caused a deep sleep to fall upon Adam, and he slept: and he took one of his ribs, and closed up the flesh instead thereof; And the rib, which the Lord God had taken from man, made he a woman, and brought her unto the man.

6. **Genesis 2:23** — And Adam said, This is now bone of my bones, and flesh of my flesh: she shall be called Woman, because she was taken out of Man.

A Note From Rick Renner

I am on a personal quest to see a "revival of the Bible" so people can establish their lives on a firm foundation that will stand strong and endure the test as end-time storm winds begin to intensify.

In order to experience a revival of the Bible in your personal life, it is important to take time each day to read, receive, and apply its truths to your life. James tells us that if we will continue in the perfect law of liberty — refusing to be forgetful hearers, but determined to be doers — we will be blessed in our ways. As you watch or listen to the programs in this series and work through this corresponding study guide, I trust you will search the Scriptures and allow the Holy Spirit to help you hear something new from God's Word that applies specifically to your life. I encourage you to be a doer of the Word He reveals to you. Whatever the cost, I assure you — it will be worth it.

> Thy words were found, and I did eat them;
> and thy word was unto me the joy and rejoicing of mine heart:
> for I am called by thy name, O Lord God of hosts.
> — Jeremiah 15:16

Your brother and friend in Jesus Christ,

Rick Renner

Unless otherwise indicated, all scripture quotations are taken from the *King James Version* of the Bible.

Scripture quotations marked (*AMPC*) are taken from the *Amplified® Bible*. Copyright © 1954, 1958, 1962, 1964, 1965, 1987 by The Lockman Foundation. Used by permission. www.Lockman.org.

Scripture quotations marked (*ESV*) are from *The Holy Bible, English Standard Version*. ESV® Text Edition: 2016. Copyright © 2001 by Crossway Bibles, a publishing ministry of Good News Publishers.

Scripture quotations marked (*NKJV*) are taken from the *New King James Version®*. Copyright © 1982 by Thomas Nelson. Used by permission. All rights reserved.

The Tragic Mistake of Moral Surrender

Copyright © 2022 by Rick Renner
P.O. Box 702040
Tulsa, OK 74170

Published by Rick Renner Ministries
www.renner.org

ISBN 13: 978-1-6803-1998-9

eBook ISBN 13: 978-1-6803-1999-6

All rights reserved. No portion of this book may be reproduced or transmitted in any form or by any means — electronic, mechanical, photocopy, recording, scanning, or other — except for brief quotations in critical reviews or articles, without the prior written permission of the Publisher.

7. **Genesis 5:2** — Male and female created he them...and called their name Adam...
8. **Genesis 3:20** —And Adam called his wife's name Eve; because she was the mother of all living.
9. **Genesis 2:24,25** — Therefore shall a man leave his father and his mother, and shall cleave unto his wife: and they shall be one flesh. And they were both naked, the man and his wife, and were not ashamed.
10. **Genesis 3:1** — Now the serpent was more subtil than any beast of the field which the Lord God had made. And he said unto the woman, Yea, hath God said, Ye shall not eat of every tree of the garden?
11. **Genesis 3:2,3** — And the woman said unto the serpent, We may eat of the fruit of the trees of the garden: But of the fruit of the tree which is in the midst of the garden, God hath said, Ye shall not eat of it, neither shall ye touch it, lest ye die.
12. **Genesis 3:4-6** — And the serpent said unto the woman, Ye shall not surely die: For God doth know that in the day ye eat thereof, then your eyes shall be opened, and ye shall be as gods, knowing good and evil. And when the woman saw that the tree was good for food, and that it was pleasant to the eyes, and a tree to be desired to make one wise, she took of the fruit thereof, and did eat, and gave also unto her husband with her; and he did eat.
13. **Genesis 3:7** — And the eyes of them both were opened, and they knew that they were naked; and they sewed fig leaves together, and made themselves aprons.
14. **Genesis 3:8-12** — And they heard the voice of the Lord God walking in the garden in the cool of the day: and Adam and his wife hid themselves from the presence of the Lord God amongst the trees of the garden. And the Lord God called unto Adam, and said unto him, Where art thou? And he said, I heard thy voice in the garden, and I was afraid, because I was naked; and I hid myself. And he said, Who told thee that thou wast naked? Hast thou eaten of the tree, whereof I commanded thee that thou shouldest not eat? And the man said, The woman whom thou gavest to be with me, she gave me of the tree, and I did eat.
15. **Romans 5:12** — Wherefore, as by one man sin entered into the world, and death by sin; and so death passed upon all men, for that all have sinned.

16. **Genesis 3:15** — And I will put enmity between thee and the woman, and between thy seed and her seed; it shall bruise thy head, and thou shalt bruise his heel.

GREEK WORDS
There are no Greek words in this lesson.

SYNOPSIS
The five lessons in this study on *The Tragic Mistake of Moral Surrender* will focus on the following topics:

- The Tragic Mistake of Moral Surrender
- Moral Surrender for Opportunity
- Moral Surrender and Embracing Inclusivity and Tolerance
- Moral Surrender for Society's Acceptance
- God's Promise to People Who Help Wandering Saints Get Back on Track

The emphasis of this lesson:

The first tragic mistake of moral surrender took place in the garden: Adam fully understood God's command, yet he disobeyed, partook of the fruit, and opened the door for Satan to flood the earth with death and destruction. But God, in His goodness, had a plan of redemption!

Do you know someone who has strayed from their faith and seems to be wandering? The Lord can use *you* to help them return to Him. "…Whoever brings back a sinner from his wandering will save his soul from death and will cover a multitude of sins" (James 5:20 *ESV*).

The first moral surrender recorded in the Bible occurred in the garden. In Genesis 2:7-9, the Word says, "And the Lord God formed man of the dust of the ground, and breathed into his nostrils the breath of life; and man became a living soul. And the Lord God planted a garden eastward in Eden; and there he put the man whom he had formed. And out of the ground made the Lord God to grow every tree that is pleasant to the sight, and good for food; the tree of life also in the midst of the garden, and the tree of knowledge of good and evil."

God Charged Adam To Protect the Garden With Vigilance

Genesis 2:15 explains, "And the Lord God took the man, and put him into the garden of Eden to dress it and to keep it." Adam was to "dress" the garden, meaning he was *to modify, cultivate, and develop it*. As good as the garden was, once it was placed into Adam's trust, God expected him to do something with it. When God gives us something, He always expects us to take it to the next level, develop it, and make it the best it can possibly be. Adam was charged with this responsibility of the garden.

Adam was also commanded to "keep" the garden. The word "keep" in Hebrew carries the idea of *vigilance*, and *protecting something from some sinister outside force*. The very fact that God used this word "keep" means He clearly communicated to Adam that there was an arch enemy out there — Satan — who would try to penetrate the garden and take it. Adam was to "keep" the garden, and safeguard it from any intruder. This was God's charge, and Adam fully understood it. God is a master communicator, and He communicated very clearly to Adam *why* he was to protect the garden.

"And the Lord God commanded the man, saying, Of every tree of the garden thou mayest freely eat: But of the tree of the knowledge of good and evil, thou shalt not eat of it: for in the day that thou eatest thereof thou shalt surely die" (Genesis 2:16,17). Notice verse 17, "…Thou shalt not eat of it: for in the day that thou eatest thereof thou shalt surely die." Disobedience in this matter would open the door and allow the devil to flood the earth with death and destruction (*see* Romans 5:14,17).

Genesis 2:18-20 continues, "And the Lord God said, It is not good that the man should be alone; I will make him an help meet for him. And out of the ground the Lord God formed every beast of the field, and every fowl of the air; and brought them unto Adam to see what he would call them: and whatsoever Adam called every living creature, that was the name thereof. And Adam gave names to all cattle, and to the fowl of the air, and to every beast of the field; but for Adam there was not found an help meet for him." Adam looked at all the animals and observed they came in pairs, but he couldn't find *his*.

"And the Lord God caused a deep sleep to fall upon Adam, and he slept: and he took one of his ribs, and closed up the flesh instead thereof; And the rib, which the Lord God had taken from man, made he a woman, and brought her unto the man" (Genesis 2:21,22). Notice, God did all of this while Adam was *sleeping*. My friend, God is working all the time, even when you're sleeping. Declare that when you go to bed at night by saying, "Lord, I know you're working, even while I'm sleeping."

A Beautiful Gift Was Presented to Adam — Eve!

While Adam slept, God "made" the woman. The word "made" means *to manufacture*. God produced this fabulous woman and "brought" her to Adam. The word "brought" carries the idea of a *magnificent presentation*. God presented this beautiful gift to Adam. "And Adam said, This is now bone of my bones, and flesh of my flesh: she shall be called Woman, because she was taken out of Man. Therefore shall a man leave his father and his mother, and shall cleave unto his wife: and they shall be one flesh. And they were both naked, the man and his wife, and were not ashamed" (Genesis 2:23-25).

What's interesting is God gave them *one* name. In the beginning, their names were not Adam and Eve — they just had *one* name. Genesis 5:2 says, "Male and female created he them…and called *their* name Adam…." They had *one* identity, and they retained it until the fall. This shows us God's original plan for unity in marriage. Eve's separate identity emerged *after* sin. She started to feel separate from Adam and his authority, and tension in the home emerged.

"Eve," the name she received *after* the fall, was given to her by Adam — not God. "And Adam called his wife's name Eve; because she was the mother of all living" (Genesis 3:20). It was Adam who called her Eve.

Satan Entered the Garden

It seems everything was fine until Satan entered the scene in Genesis 3:1 which says, "Now the serpent was more subtil than any beast of the field which the Lord God had made. And he said unto the woman, Yea, hath God said, Ye shall not eat of every tree of the garden?"

Satan didn't approach Adam, he approached Eve. Why? Because Adam clearly heard from God about the *real* matter — which was not the tree, but rather, obedience. Adam's job was to keep the devil *out* of the garden, and he clearly understood that. Eve was not there in the beginning when God first gave this charge to Adam.

"And the woman said unto the serpent, We may eat of the fruit of the trees of the garden: But of the fruit of the tree which is in the midst of the garden, God hath said, Ye shall not eat of it, neither shall ye touch it, lest ye die" (Genesis 3:2,3). Notice those words, "…Neither shall ye touch it." If you go back to Genesis 2, that's not what God said in His charge to Adam. What *did* He say? "And the Lord God commanded the man, saying, Of every tree of the garden thou mayest freely eat: But of the tree of the knowledge of good and evil, thou shalt not eat of it: for in the day that thou eatest thereof thou shalt surely die" (Genesis 2:16,17). Eve *added* the words, "…Neither shall ye touch it…" (Genesis 3:3).

It appears that Eve perceived there was something poisonous about the tree. She did not understand the main issue was obedience or disobedience to the command of God. She may have thought, *We can't even touch it because there's something fatal in the tree itself. It's poisonous.* Eve did not understand, and her ignorance opened the door for the devil to lead her off track and deceive her. The Bible says, "My people are destroyed for lack of knowledge…" (Hosea 4:6). The devil always operates where there is ignorance. Eve took the blame, but as the head of his home, Adam should have clearly communicated to his wife, just as God had clearly communicated to him. But Adam didn't.

Genesis 3:4-6 continues, "And the serpent said unto the woman, Ye shall not surely die: For God doth know that in the day ye eat thereof, then your eyes shall be opened, and ye shall be as gods, knowing good and evil. And when the woman saw that the tree was good for food, and that it was pleasant to the eyes, and a tree to be desired to make one wise, she took of the fruit thereof, and did eat, and gave also unto her husband with her; and he did eat."

Adam ate the fruit fully understanding what he was doing. That single decision opened the door for death and destruction to enter the earth. He knew that now Eve had partaken of the fruit, she was going to die spiritually, and eventually she would die physically. If he did not *join* her, he would *lose* her. Adam was alive unto God and now Eve was in sin, which meant they were instantly *unequally yoked*. Fully understanding what he was doing, Adam let down his guard, and made the tragic mistake of moral surrender. He followed his wife, partook of the fruit, and disobeyed God's command.

What Influences People Today To Morally Surrender?

Similarly, and sadly, when children raised in Christian homes wander from the faith, some parents give in and accommodate the compromise because they don't want to be separated from their children. Siblings do the same thing: They love each other, yet when a brother or sister embraces wrong things, their siblings may cave in and justify themselves by thinking, *Maybe what they're doing is okay after all.*

When your friends adapt to the end-time culture surrounding them and you know that if you remain solid on the Word of God you'll no longer be friends, what will you do? If you can't bear the thought of being separated from the friends you love, you may be tempted to yield to the same areas of compromise they have yielded to. Tragically, friends cave in to friends; siblings cave in to siblings; and parents cave in to their children.

So many believers today feel the pressure of society, and the brunt of it comes against them through the media, newspaper, courts, and education. Society tells people to change what they believe about sexuality and morality. People feel the pressure of society against them, and they're told that if they don't change the way they think and what they endorse, they'll be "canceled."

There's nothing tolerant about our society whatsoever. Today's society claims to be tolerant of everything, but they're actually only tolerant of those who *agree* with them. If you have an opposing view or an open mind that doesn't agree with everything this end-time society says, they'll just outright "cancel" you and try to eliminate you from having any influence.

Because some people can't deal with the pressure coming against them from the media, courts, Hollywood, education, and even their family, they cave in and commit the tragic mistake of moral surrender. It began with Adam in the Garden of Eden: Eve ate the fruit first, then understanding what he was doing, Adam followed her and partook of the forbidden fruit as well. He failed to be a leader, and caved in to the situation.

Friend, when you cave in to the pressures around you, it opens a door for tragedy to come into your life. However, if you stay on target, when the people who have veered off course need help, they'll come back to you. But if you cave in *with* them, they won't have you to come to for help. Stay on track and be an example and a friend they can run to when they get into trouble.

'By One Man Sin Entered the World'

Genesis 3:8-12 continues, "And they heard the voice of the Lord God walking in the garden in the cool of the day: and Adam and his wife hid themselves from the presence of the Lord God amongst the trees of the garden. And the Lord God called unto Adam, and said unto him, Where art thou? And he said, I heard thy voice in the garden, and I was afraid, because I was naked; and I hid myself. And he said, Who told thee that thou wast naked? Hast thou eaten of the tree, whereof I commanded thee that thou shouldest not eat? And the man said, The woman whom thou gavest to be with me, she gave me of the tree, and I did eat."

In Genesis 3:12, Adam began to shift the blame. First, he blamed God by saying, "It's the woman *You* gave me…." Secondly, he said, "*She* gave it to me to eat." Instead of owning up to his responsibility, he shifted the blame to God *and* to his wife. Today, when people cave in to pressure, they blame all kinds of things: Their spouse, their friends, the church, the courts, school, Hollywood, or social media.

Adam was the head of his home, the garden, and the human race. Regardless of the part his wife played in the sin, God held Adam accountable. Romans 5:12 says, "Wherefore, as by one man sin entered into the world, and death by sin; and so death passed upon all men, for that all have sinned."

By *one man* sin entered the world, and that "one man" was Adam. When Adam caved in, the door opened for sin, death, and destruction to flood into the garden, the world, and the human race. All of this happened because *one man* made the tragic mistake of moral surrender. But the Lord promised that He would fix it, and He did!

Redeemed!

God spoke to the serpent and prophesied, "And I will put enmity between thee and the woman, and between thy seed and her seed; it shall bruise thy head, and thou shalt bruise his heel" (Genesis 3:15). God prophesied that the devil would kill Jesus, but Jesus would bruise Satan's head in the resurrection. It was the plan of redemption, which God prophesied from the very beginning!

My friend, God is so good! If you have made the tragic mistake of moral surrender, God will put a plan of redemption into action *if* you have a heart that is willing to repent, and *if* you'll ask God to help you. He will turn it all around!

If you know someone who has wandered from their faith, there is something you can do to help! We'll discover what that is in our next lesson.

STUDY QUESTIONS

> **Study to shew thyself approved unto God, a workman that needeth not to be ashamed, rightly dividing the word of truth.**
> — 2 Timothy 2:15

1. If you surrender to the seductive ways of our society, it will cost you. What are some things you can do to fortify yourself against the trap of moral surrender? Consider First John 2:15-17 and Proverbs 1:10-33.
2. According to John 8:44, who is the father of lies? And in Genesis 3:4 and 5, what did this father of lies say to Eve in the garden? Was that true? According to First Timothy 2:14, what was the result?
3. Adam was charged to vigilantly guard the garden. Likewise, you are to stay vigilant because there is an enemy who walks about seeking whom he may devour. Let him know he may not devour you or your family! First Peter 5:8 says, "Be sober, be vigilant; because your adversary the devil, as a roaring lion, walketh about, seeking whom he may devour." In what ways are you standing watch over your family?

PRACTICAL APPLICATION

> **But be ye doers of the word, and not hearers only, deceiving your own selves.**
> — James 1:22

1. In order to be strong and not cave in to the pressures or the people who surround you, it's vital that you saturate yourself in the Word of God daily. His Word is truth! When you walk in truth, and live without compromising biblical principles, you'll be a beacon of light in this dark world. And you can help restore people who need to return to God (*see* Galatians 6:1). Ask the Holy Spirit to strengthen you as you live according to *the truth* (*see* John 17:17; Psalm 33:4; 3 John 4).

2. Satan operates where there is ignorance. Hosea 4:6 says, "My people are destroyed for lack of knowledge." Have you experienced a situation in your life that opened the door to the devil because you were ignorant about something? What did you learn from it?
3. Do you know someone who has wandered morally? It may be your friend, parent, sibling, spouse, child, or grandchild. Be encouraged — you can be used by God to bring them back on track. Remain steadfast in your walk with the Lord and your prayers for them, and God will turn it around! Consider Ephesians 6:18 and James 5:16 (*AMPC*). Pray fervently now for the people in your life who have morally surrendered.

LESSON 2

TOPIC
Moral Surrender For Opportunity

SCRIPTURES
1. **Genesis 13:10,11** — Lot lifted up his eyes, and beheld all the plain of Jordan, that it was well watered every where, before the Lord destroyed Sodom and Gomorrah, even as the garden of the Lord, like the land of Egypt, as thou comest unto Zoar. Then Lot chose him all the plain of Jordan; and Lot journeyed east: and they separated themselves the one from the other.
2. **Genesis 13:12** — Abram dwelled in the land of Canaan, and Lot dwelled in the cities of the plain, and pitched his tent toward Sodom.
3. **Genesis 13:13** — But the men of Sodom were wicked and sinners before the Lord exceedingly.
4. **Genesis 18:1,2** — And the Lord appeared unto him in the plains of Mamre: and he sat in the tent door in the heat of the day. And he lift up his eyes and looked, and, lo, three men stood by him: and when he saw them, he ran to meet them from the tent door, and bowed himself toward the ground.
5. **Genesis 18:16,17** — And the men rose up from thence, and looked toward Sodom: and Abraham went with them to bring them on the

way. And the Lord said, Shall I hide from Abraham that thing which I do.

6. **Psalm 34:15** — The eyes of the Lord are upon the righteous, and his ears are open unto their cry.
7. **Genesis 18:20-22** — And the Lord said, Because the cry of Sodom and Gomorrah is great, and because their sin is very grievous; I will go down now, and see whether they have done altogether according to the cry of it, which is come unto me; and if not, I will know. And the men turned their faces from thence, and went toward Sodom: but Abraham stood yet before the Lord.
8. **Genesis 19:1** — And there came two angels to Sodom at even; and Lot sat in the gate of Sodom: and Lot seeing them rose up to meet them; and he bowed himself with his face toward the ground.
9. **Genesis 19:2** — And he said, Behold now, my lords, turn in, I pray you, into your servant's house, and tarry all night, and wash your feet, and ye shall rise up early, and go on your ways. And they said, Nay; but we will abide in the street all night.
10. **Genesis 19:3-5** — And he pressed upon them greatly; and they turned in unto him, and entered into his house; and he made them a feast, and did bake unleavened bread, and they did eat. But before they lay down, the men of the city, even the men of Sodom, compassed the house round, both old and young, all the people from every quarter: And they called unto Lot, and said unto him, Where are the men which came in to thee this night? bring them out unto us, that we may know them.
11. **Genesis 19:6,7** — And Lot went out at the door unto them, and shut the door after him, And said, I pray you, brethren, do not so wickedly.
12. **Genesis 19:8** — Behold now, I have two daughters which have not known man; let me, I pray you, bring them out unto you, and do ye to them as is good in your eyes: only unto these men do nothing; for therefore came they under the shadow of my roof.
13. **Genesis 19:9** — …And they said again, This one fellow came in to sojourn, and he will needs be a judge: now will we deal worse with thee, than with them. And they pressed sore upon the man, even Lot, and came near to break the door.
14. **Genesis 19:10,11** — But the men put forth their hand, and pulled Lot into the house to them, and shut to the door. And they smote the

men that were at the door of the house with blindness, both small and great: so that they wearied themselves to find the door.
15. **Genesis 19:12** — And the men said unto Lot, Hast thou here any besides? son in law, and thy sons, and thy daughters, and whatsoever thou hast in the city, bring them out of this place.
16. **Genesis 19:13** — For we will destroy this place, because the cry of them is waxen great before the face of the Lord; and the Lord hath sent us to destroy it.
17. **Genesis 19:14** — And Lot went out, and spake unto his sons in law, which married his daughters, and said, Up, get you out of this place; for the Lord will destroy this city. But he seemed as one that mocked unto his sons in law.
18. **Genesis 19:15** — And when the morning arose, then the angels hastened Lot, saying, Arise, take thy wife, and thy two daughters, which are here; lest thou be consumed in the iniquity of the city.
19. **Genesis 19:16** — And while he lingered, the men laid hold upon his hand, and upon the hand of his wife, and upon the hand of his two daughters; the Lord being merciful unto him: and they brought him forth, and set him without the city.
20. **2 Peter 2:9** — The Lord knoweth how to deliver the godly out of temptations…

GREEK WORDS

1. "deliver" — ῥύομαι (*rhuomai*): to snatch out of danger just in the nick of time

SYNOPSIS

The emphasis of this lesson:

Lot surrendered morally and compromised for the sake of opportunity. But because his uncle Abraham drew near to the Lord and interceded, Lot was delivered, and snatched out of danger just in time. Likewise, if you will draw near to the Lord on behalf of those you're concerned about, God's delivering power will go to work on their behalf!

Do you know someone who made the tragic mistake of moral surrender, and now their decisions are so unlike the real *them* it's hard for you to even grasp? Are they embracing things they would have never embraced before?

How could they veer so far off track? Has space developed between the two of you because they've changed so much? Abraham and Lot spent years together, yet when they separated, Lot began to morally surrender and compromise.

A Little History About Lot

Lot had a great beginning. When Abraham and Sarah began their walk of faith, Lot was with them. When Abraham announced his conversion to God, Lot was there. When Abraham and Sarah left Haran and began to follow God into the land of Canaan, Lot was with them. And when Abraham entered into the land of Canaan and he saw all the giants there, again, Lot was with him.

When Abraham built an altar and dedicated himself to God, Lot was with him. When Abraham and Sarah went into the land of Egypt, Lot was there accompanying them. Lot witnessed the hand of God at work in his family and saw how God protected and blessed Abraham.

Lot was with Abraham through many things — at first. But then *something happened*. Abraham and Lot became so blessed and their substance was so great that they couldn't dwell together any longer.

Where Lot's Mistake of Moral Surrender Began

To avoid strife between their herdsmen, Abraham offered Lot the first choice of where he wanted to live…and that is where Lot's mistake of moral surrender began. Genesis 13:10,11 says, "Lot lifted up his eyes, and beheld all the plain of Jordan, that it was well watered every where, before the Lord destroyed Sodom and Gomorrah, even as the garden of the Lord, like the land of Egypt, as thou comest unto Zoar. Then Lot chose him all the plain of Jordan; and Lot journeyed east: and they separated themselves the one from the other."

Lot separated himself from his spiritual father, and immediately began to make bad decisions. Abraham stayed in the land of Canaan; he camped in the promise of God. But Lot began to lift up his eyes and look at the *opportunity* in Sodom and Gomorrah.

From Lot's vantage point, he could see the beautiful Jordan valley in front of him and he "beheld" it. The word "beheld" is translated from a Hebrew word which means *to be mesmerized*. Lot was mesmerized and captivated by the land he saw before him. In many ways that area was very similar to Ur of the Chaldees, which they had left. Lot's heart strings were tugged to go back to what he had been delivered from.

Genesis 13:12 tells us, "Abram dwelled in the land of Canaan, and Lot dwelled in the cities of the plain, and pitched his tent toward Sodom." The cities of Sodom and Gomorrah were extremely prosperous, and the idea of going there represented great financial opportunity. It was also common knowledge that the men there were exceedingly wicked before the presence of the Lord. Lot was not ignorant about the cities of Sodom and Gomorrah.

Sodom and Gomorrah Are Mentioned Throughout the Bible

In Deuteronomy 29:23, Moses said Sodom and Gomorrah were so horrible that when God destroyed them nothing would grow there. Isaiah mentioned Sodom and Gomorrah several times, and in Isaiah 3:9, he specifically cited that their sin was shameless and out in the open.

Jeremiah 23:14 states that Sodom and Gomorrah were filled with adultery and lies. Ezekiel 16:49 adds that the cities of Sodom and Gomorrah were filled with pride. And Amos 4:1-12 declared that if other cities did not repent, they would be judged just like Sodom and Gomorrah.

Jesus spoke about Sodom and Gomorrah on several occasions. Luke 17:28 and 29 tells us Sodom was affluent and prosperous. The people there ate, drank, bought, sold, planted, and built their lives the way *they* wanted to build them.

Second Peter 2:4-11 tells us God destroyed the cities completely because of their lasciviousness. Jude verse 7 says the people of Sodom went after "strange flesh," which is a description of sexual perversion. And Revelation 11:7,8 describes Sodom as the symbol of sin and all kinds of defilement.

Lot 'Pitched His Tent Toward Sodom'

Lot walked with his father of faith, Abraham, and he knew God. So what in the world was a man like Lot doing moving toward Sodom and Gomorrah? The answer is — he was *mesmerized* by the opportunity there.

Luxurious Sodom was loaded with wealth and business opportunities. Lot walked the hard road of faith with his uncle Abraham for a long time, and the idea of going somewhere a little easier was very alluring to his flesh. Initially, Lot lived *outside* Sodom and Gomorrah in the plain of Jordan, but the Bible says he "…pitched his tent toward Sodom" (Genesis 13:12).

Sitting under his tent he could see the lights of the city, hear the sounds of the city, and smell the smells of the city. Like a magnet attracts metal, the city began to speak to his flesh, draw him, and tantalize him to move closer and closer until finally he found himself living *right in the middle* of Sodom.

God Heard the Cry of the Sin of Sodom and Gomorrah

Lot could see with his own eyes the sin that filled the city. "But the men of Sodom were wicked and sinners before the Lord exceedingly" (Genesis 13:13). But because opportunities were there, Lot coaxed himself into believing it was alright for him to move there. It was a tragic mistake of moral surrender. Lot surrendered *morally* for the sake of *opportunity*.

The sin in Sodom and Gomorrah was so horrible that God could hear the cry of it in Heaven. Genesis 18:1,2 says, "And the Lord appeared unto him in the plains of Mamre: and he sat in the tent door in the heat of the day; And he lift up his eyes and looked, and, lo, three men stood by him: and when he saw them, he ran to meet them from the tent door, and bowed himself toward the ground." We know from the text that two of these men were angels and one was the Lord. Abraham and Sarah prepared and served them a delectable meal.

Genesis 18:16,17 declares, "And the men [the two angels] rose up from thence, and looked toward Sodom: and Abraham went with them to bring them on the way. And the Lord said, Shall I hide from Abraham that thing which I do."

But Abraham Stood Yet Before the Lord!

The angels were about to be dispatched into Sodom and into Gomorrah to see about the great cry coming from the cities that God heard in Heaven. Scripture tells us there are two things God can actually *hear*. First of all, He hears *the cry of His people*. Psalm 34:15 says, "The eyes of the Lord are upon the righteous, and his ears are open unto their cry." When God's people cry out, He comes down to deliver them.

Secondly, God can hear *the cry of sin*, and the more grievous the sin, the louder the cry. Genesis 18:20-22 declares, "And the Lord said, Because the cry of Sodom and Gomorrah is great, and because their sin is very grievous; I will go down now, and see whether they have done altogether according to the cry of it, which is come unto me; and if not, I will know. And the men turned their faces from thence, and went toward Sodom: but Abraham stood yet before the Lord."

They were being dispatched into the city of Sodom to investigate and to see if the sin was as grievous as it sounded. But Abraham stood before the Lord to intercede for Lot.

My friends, when people are in trouble, it's time for us to do what Abraham did and stand before the Lord and draw near. He knew when the angels arrived in the cities and saw the decadence, the sin, and the perversion — they would destroy it. Abraham didn't just wash his hands and say, "There's nothing I can do for my nephew." He drew near to the Lord and interceded on behalf of his family. He knew if he did not intercede, his family who lived in Sodom would be in serious trouble.

Lot Fell So Far Morally That He Sat in the Gate of Sodom As One of Its Leaders

Over time, Lot had blended into the environment of Sodom to the point that he sat in the gate as one of the leaders of the city. "And there came two angels to Sodom at even; and Lot sat in the gate of Sodom: and Lot seeing them rose up to meet them; and he bowed himself with his face toward the ground" (Genesis 19:1). The angels found Lot sitting in the gate of Sodom! This shows how far he had sunk morally because those who sat in the gate of the city were Sodom's *leaders*. They were the business people and the public servants who carried out necessary transactions to ensure the city was successful.

Lot spoke to the two angels and said, "…Behold now, my lords, turn in, I pray you, into your servant's house, and tarry all night, and wash your feet, and ye shall rise up early, and go on your ways. And they said, Nay; but we will abide in the street all night" (Genesis 19:2).

Notice the words, "...Tarry all night." They came to the city to see what was happening there, not to stay all night with Lot. But Lot knew if they stayed in the streets at night, they would see evil things taking place such as every kind of sexual perversion. Lot knew that if the angels saw these things, they would destroy the city, and because he loved the city of Sodom and didn't want it to be destroyed, he begged them to stay in his house all night.

The Angels Rejected Lot's Invitation

Lot insisted the angels come to his home. "And he pressed upon them greatly; and they turned in unto him, and entered into his house; and he made them a feast, and did bake unleavened bread, and they did eat. But before they lay down, the men of the city, even the men of Sodom, compassed the house round, both old and young, all the people from every quarter: And they called unto Lot, and said unto him, Where are the men which came in to thee this night? bring them out unto us, that we may know them" (Genesis 19:3-5).

The word, "know" means *to sexually know*, and here we find a disgusting picture. Men of all ages — old and young, from every sector of the city — surrounded the house, and in a lustful rage they demanded that the two visitors be brought out to them so they could forcibly have sex with them. Sexual perversion was so widespread in Sodom that both the old and the young were involved in it.

With their lust burning out of control, their intent was to take the new "men" (the angels from the Lord) and sexually "know" them, or gang rape them. Genesis 19:6,7 says, "And Lot went out at the door unto them, and shut the door after him, And said, I pray you, brethren, do not so wickedly."

Lot looked into the faces of these perverted, exceedingly wicked sinners and called them "brethren." Keep in mind, this is the same Lot who once walked in faith with his uncle Abraham. He previously helped Abraham build altars unto God. But he had become so brainwashed by living continuously in sin's environment, that he looked into the face of these perverted individuals and called them "brethren."

Lot was so completely compromised in his thinking, He said to the Sodomites, "Behold now, I have two daughters which have not known man; let me, I pray you, bring them out unto you, and do ye to them as is good in your eyes: only unto these men do nothing; for therefore came they under the shadow of my roof" (Genesis 19:8). Lot was so seared and reprobate in his thinking, he said, "It's not good that you would rape these angels, but I do have two girls who have never known men; you can have them and do to them whatever you wish." *Clearly, there is nothing right about that at all!*

When the Sodomites Pressed — the Angels Took Charge

The Sodomites said to Lot, "…This one fellow came in to sojourn, and he will needs be a judge: now will we deal worse with thee, than with them. And they pressed sore upon the man, even Lot, and came near to break the door." (Genesis 19:9).

The Sodomites basically said, "Who do you think *you* are telling us what is right and wrong? *You* of all people are going to judge us? When we're done, we're going to do worse to *you* then we do to those two men." Wow! Lot had so blended into the environment of Sodom that he lost his voice of authority, and when he tried to speak with moral authority, the men of Sodom didn't take him seriously.

Genesis 19:10 and 11 declares, "But the men [the angels] put forth their hand, and pulled Lot into the house to them, and shut to the door. And they smote the men that were at the door of the house with blindness, both small and great: so that they wearied themselves to find the door." The angels took matters into their own hands and struck all the Sodomites with blindness so they couldn't find Lot or their way into Lot's house, and so they couldn't escape the city when destruction fell.

The angels then voiced their warning and intent for the city: "And the men [angels] said unto Lot, Hast thou here any besides? *son in law*, and thy sons, and thy daughters, and whatsoever thou hast in the city, bring them out of this place" (Genesis 19:12). Apparently, Lot's daughters were married, yet had never engaged in sexual intercourse with their husbands. The angels continued, "For we will destroy this place, because of the cry of them is waxen great before the face of the Lord; and the Lord hath sent us to destroy it" (Genesis 19:13).

Judgment Was About To Fall, But Lot 'Lingered'

"And Lot went out, and spake unto his sons in law, which married his daughters, and said, Up, get you out of this place; for the Lord will destroy this city. But he seemed as one that mocked unto his sons in law" (Genesis 19:14). Lot spoke words of truth and deliverance, but his sons-in-law had never seen him take a righteous stand, and they mocked him for it.

"And when the morning arose, then the angels hastened Lot, saying, Arise, take thy wife, and thy two daughters, which are here; lest thou be consumed in the iniquity of the city" (Genesis 19:15). The angels hurried Lot and basically said, "Come on! Get moving! You've got to get out of here!" Notice, the sons-in-law did not follow.

"And while he lingered, the men [angels] laid hold upon his hand, and upon the hand of his wife, and upon the hand of his two daughters; the Lord being merciful unto him: and they brought him forth, and set him without the city" (Genesis 19:16).

Lot knew judgment was about to fall, but he was hoping that it wouldn't *really* happen. So he *lingered*; he wasn't moving. But God was still merciful to Lot. The angels took him by the hand, and his wife's hand, and the hand of his two daughters, and they mercifully set Lot and his family outside the city.

Because Abraham Prayed, Lot and His Family Were Snatched Out of Danger Just in Time

Fire and brimstone then fell upon Sodom and Gomorrah, and God overthrew the cities of the plain. But Lot and his family were delivered. When you look at the story, it looks like Lot and his family weren't too interested in being delivered. He had tragically surrendered all of his morals for the sake of opportunity.

Lot didn't even have the sense to walk out of a mess when God was trying to deliver him. Then why did God deliver him? Because Abraham, his uncle, drew near to the Lord, stood before the Lord, and interceded on his behalf. And that is why Second Peter 2:9 tells us, "The Lord knoweth how to deliver the godly out of temptations...."

The word "deliver" is the Greek word *rhuomai*, and means *to snatch out of danger just in the nick of time*. Because of Abraham's intercession, God snatched Lot and his family out of harm's way just in the nick of time before judgment fell.

Just like Abraham interceded for Lot, if *you* will draw near to the Lord on behalf of those you know who have veered morally, God's delivering power will go to work on *their* behalf!

STUDY QUESTIONS

> Study to shew thyself approved unto God, a workman that needeth not to be ashamed, rightly dividing the word of truth.
> — 2 Timothy 2:15

"Ye therefore, beloved, seeing ye know these things before, beware lest ye also, being led away with the error of the wicked, fall from your own steadfastness" (2 Peter 3:17).

1. Righteous Lot pitched his tent toward Sodom and allowed the wickedness of the city to permeate his heart and life. His morals literally eroded away as he blended in with Sodom for the sake of opportunity. There is a principle of proximity: When you situate yourself too close to evil, it's likely to cause you to fall. What can you do to create space between yourself and the lure of the world? (*See* Second Corinthians 6:14-18; Second Peter 3:17; and First Thessalonians 5:22,23.)
2. According to Second Peter 2:6, what does Sodom and Gomorrah's destruction reveal to us about what will happen at the end of the age?
3. The Lord heard Abraham's prayer for Lot, and He hears *your* prayers for those you are concerned about.
   - "…Before they call, I will answer; and while they are yet speaking, I will hear" (Isaiah 65:24).
   - "He shall call upon me and I will answer him…" (Psalm 91:15).
   - "Then you will call upon Me, and you will come and pray to Me, and I will hear *and* heed you" (Jeremiah 29:12).

What additional Scriptures can you stand on regarding your loved one who has morally wandered? (Consider Isaiah 49:25; Acts 16:31; and Isaiah 43:5-8.)

PRACTICAL APPLICATION

> But be ye doers of the word, and not hearers only, deceiving your own selves.
> —James 1:22

1. God "...delivered just Lot, vexed with the filthy conversation of the wicked: (For that righteous man dwelling among them, in seeing and hearing, vexed his righteous soul from day to day with their unlawful deeds)" (2 Peter 2:7,8). Lot was worn out by the filthy behavior of the Sodomites that he was exposed to daily. Their lack of moral standards tortured his righteous soul. Is there an area in your life that opens the door for you to see and hear evil things day after day? How has that exposure impacted you? What can you do to change it?

2. There's something you can do to help people who have made the tragic mistake of moral surrender get back on track. Who are the people you know who really need help in this area right now? Take time right now to stand in the gap for them before the Lord like Abraham did for Lot. (Consider Hebrews 4:16; Ezekiel 22:30; Romans 8:26,27; and First John 5:14,15.)

3. Have you compromised morally in spite of the fact that you know better? Did you justify your choices because of the "gain" they would produce? God's mercy is extended to you to deliver you. Come to the Father in Jesus' name and repent for your mistakes. Consecrate your life afresh to Him. He's waiting with open arms. (*See* John 3:17; First John 1:9; and Second Corinthians 5:17.)

LESSON 3

TOPIC

Moral Surrender and Embracing Inclusivity and Tolerance

SCRIPTURES

1. **Revelation 2:13** — I know thy works, and where thou dwellest, even where Satan's seat is: and thou holdest fast my name, and hast not

denied my faith, even in those days wherein Antipas was my faithful martyr, who was slain among you, where Satan dwelleth.
2. **Revelation 2:14** — But I have a few things against thee, because thou hast there them that hold the doctrine of Balaam, who taught Balac to cast a stumblingblock before the children of Israel, to eat things sacrificed unto idols, and to commit fornication.
3. **Numbers 25:1-3** — And Israel abode in Shittim, and the people began to commit whoredom with the daughters of Moab. And they called the people unto the sacrifices of their gods: and the people did eat, and bowed down to their gods. And Israel joined himself unto Baalpeor: and the anger of the Lord was kindled against Israel.
4. **Revelation 2:15** — So hast thou also them that hold the doctrine of the Nicolaitanes, which thing I hate.

GREEK WORDS

1. "my martyr" — ὁ μάρτυς μου (*ho martus mou*): a witness summoned to testify in a court of law; connected to the idea of suffering because if a person was called to be a witness, he was required to be faithful to the truth regardless of any possible acts of retribution that might be carried out against him by those who opposed his witness or who wished to suppress the truth; when an individual was summoned to be a "witness," it was understood that it could place him or his loved ones in jeopardy; to be a "witness" required the highest level of integrity and commitment, as well as a willingness to sacrifice oneself or one's status to uphold the truth; a very real possibility was that a person could pay a high price for being a *faithful* witness
2. "slain" — ἀποκτείνω (*apokteino*): pictures the abrupt taking away of a person's life; a brutal, grisly, and gruesome death
3. "I have" — ἔχω (*echo*): I have or I hold
4. "against" — κατὰ (*kata*): a strong sense of a strike against them
5. "hold" — κρατοῦντας (*kratountas*): a powerful grip and refusal to let go
6. "stumblingblock" — σκάνδαλον (*skandalon*): a trap used to catch an animal
7. "Nicolaitans" — Νικόλαος (*Nikolaos*): to conquer and subdue people; one who conquers and subdues people
8. "hate" — μισέω (*miseo*): to hate, to abhor, or to find utterly repulsive; a deep-seated animosity; intense hatred; repugnance; something that

causes one to feel disgust, repulsion; a deep-seated aversion; not just dislike, it is actual hatred

SYNOPSIS

The emphasis of this lesson:

There was a trend in the church in Pergamum to be more "inclusive and tolerant" of others. Sound familiar? The pressure today to embrace "inclusivity and tolerance" is real. The problem is: Where sin is tolerated, separation unto Christ is ignored, and the need for repentance is disregarded, the result is a weakened version of Christianity that pulls the plug on the power of the Gospel.

When your child, grandchild, or friend veers from their faith, starts going in a different direction, and makes the tragic mistake of moral surrender, how should you respond? The worst thing you can do is cave in to pressure and follow them. It's vital that you stay on target and remain anchored in the Word of God, because a day will come when they will look for help. If you abandon biblical principles, you will not be able to help them. As noted in our previous lesson, if you draw near to the Lord in intercession, God will deliver them because you prayed!

If You Don't Comply With Inclusivity and Tolerance, Today's Society Tries To "Cancel" You

Society tells us, "You need to be inclusive and tolerant of everybody." The idea is that if you're uncompromising when it comes to what you believe, then you are "narrow-minded and bigoted." But, my friend, the Bible is absolute truth. It doesn't mean we have to be disapproving of everybody, but we are not to abandon what the Bible says!

If we appear to be intolerant or not inclusive of everyone, it's because we choose to stick with living according to the Bible. Jesus died for everyone, and we love all people — but we're not tolerant of *everything*. Even if people say we're narrow-minded, intolerant, or bigoted, we must choose to live according to God's Word.

There was a trend in the church in Pergamum to tone it down, lower the bar, and be more inclusive and more tolerant of others (*see* Revelation 2). The reason for this compromise was so Christians in Pergamum would be perceived in a better light and not be persecuted. That's exactly what we are dealing with today! The Bible is so relevant! In fact, if you don't agree with today's society, they will do their best to "cancel" you. They even have a name — "cancel culture."

Persecution in a Place Jesus Called 'Satan's Seat'

The church in Pergamum was suffering great persecution when Jesus said, "I know thy works, and where thou dwellest, even where Satan's seat is" (Revelation 2:13). The city of Pergamum was an evil city filled with demonic activity and many temples to false gods, that it really was the seat of Satan. There was a huge altar in Pergamum called the Throne of Zeus. From that throne, which sat on the edge of the upper city, smoke billowed into the air 24 hours a day.

It's interesting that it was also the seat of the Proconsul — the government of all of Asia. And from that high and lofty place, demonic powers began to impact the entire region. Jesus informed the believers, "You're living where Satan's seat is." But isn't it wonderful that Jesus knows where we live and everything we're facing?

Speaking to the church of Pergamum, Jesus continued, "…And thou holdest fast my name, and hast not denied my faith…" (Revelation 2:13). He implied the believers had an opportunity to turn loose of His Name, deny His faith, and back off of their uncompromising position. But they didn't deny Him or walk away.

Revelation 2:13 concludes, "…Even in those days wherein Antipas was my faithful martyr, who was slain among you, where Satan dwelleth". The words "in those days" are very important because Jesus was pointing to a specific number of days, and it was actually a very prolonged period of persecution. Jesus understood when it began, and how long it lasted.

A Man Who Wouldn't Violate His Convictions

Jesus knows everything you're dealing with. He said specifically, "…Even in those days wherin Antipas was My faithful martyr, who was slain among you…" (Revelation 2:13). Antipas was probably the first pastor of the church in Pergamum. Understand that he was indeed a person, but his name symbolically described what the people in Pergamum generally thought of Christians, which is very important.

The word "Antipas" is a compound of two words, the word "anti," which means *against*, and the word "pas," which means *everything*. When you compound the two words, the name Antipas means *one who seems to simply be against everything*. It carries the idea of a person who is *antisocial, contrary, noncompliant, intolerant, narrow-minded, non-conformist, inflexible, obstinate*, or *uncompromising*. That describes what the people of Pergamum thought about Antipas — a man who would not lower the bar and would not violate his convictions.

The people of Pergamum didn't just think *Antipas* was *against everything* — they thought *all* Christians were *against everything*. From their perspective, Christians appeared to be *antisocial, contrary, non-compliant, intolerant, narrow-minded, non-conformist, inflexible, obstinate*, and *uncompromising*. The pagan world around them said, "Why can't you be more inclusive? Why can't you be more tolerant? Why do you have to be so uncompromising in what you believe?" Do you see how relevant this is when it comes to what we're dealing with in the world today?

Notice that Jesus calls Antipas "my faithful martyr," translated from the Greek words *ho martus mou*, which literally means *the martyr of mine, my faithful one*. It carries the idea that Jesus was proud of Antipas because he was unbending and uncompromising. Jesus basically said, "I'm proud of him; he's the *witness* of mine; the faithful one of mine." Antipas' unwavering, uncompromising life was an example for believers both then and now.

How Much Are You Willing To Sacrifice To Walk in Truth?

The word "witness" is a translation of the Greek word *martus*. It depicts *a witness summoned to testify in a court of law*; and is connected to the idea of suffering. If a person was called to be a witness, he was required to be faithful to the truth regardless of any possible acts of retribution that might be carried out against him by those who opposed his witness or who wished to suppress the truth.

When an individual was summoned to be a "witness," they understood that it could place their loved ones in jeopardy. To be a "witness" required the highest level of integrity and commitment, as well as a willingness to sacrifice oneself or one's status to uphold the truth. A person could pay a high price for being *a faithful witness*. In other words, "If you stick with what you're saying, we're going to oppose you, and in some way or another, we're going to 'cancel' you. We're going to eliminate you."

And we are in the same position today. If you stick with the truth, if you're uncompromising and unbending in what you believe, the world around you will do their best to eliminate you or to "cancel" you. That's what we're dealing with in the world today!

Revelation 2:13 goes on to say, "Antipas…was slain among you…." The word "slain" is the horrible Greek word *apokteino*, which pictures *the abrupt taking away of a person's life; a brutal, grisly, and gruesome death*. The words "among you" in Greek picture *right in your midst*, which means Antipas was martyred in a public location where the entire city was aware of the hideous event. He suffered a horrible death!

Let's carry this into our contemporary times and what we're facing in society today. If you hold fast to the truth, social media will try to publicly defile you, eliminate you, laugh at you, and "cancel" you. Everyone is aware when social media suddenly turns on you. Everyone sees it because it happens *right in our midst*.

The Brutal Death of a Faithful Witness

Antipas' death was *grisly*, *brutal*, and *gruesome*. On the Acropolis of Pergamum stood a huge idol — a bronze bull. It was hollow on the inside with a door on its side. The bronze bull was used multiple times for sacrifices in the history of the city of Pergamum — not just for Antipas — but it was always used for believers. The bull was a symbol of the highest sacrifice they could offer to their gods.

Human sacrifices were bound and thrown inside the bronze bull. The door was then shut and locked. A fire was then set ablaze under the belly of the bull that literally cooked the believer to death. There were musical pipes in the head of the bull, so when a person cried out in pain from inside the bull, rather than hearing the cries and screams of the sufferer, their voice would go through the pipes and make it sound like *the bull* was literally coming to life.

When the victim was fully burned, the door on the side of the bull was opened and the bones were removed to be cut into pieces, polished, and turned into beads to be worn as jewelry. Indeed it was a *brutal*, *grisly*, and *gruesome death*. But that is the death that Antipas experienced because he was uncompromising and inflexible when it came to his faith and what he believed — he refused to let go of truth.

Christians Were Viewed as Being Against Everything

In general, Christians were viewed as "Antipas," as being *against everything*. For example, they refused to participate in the circus because of the horrific treatment of human beings that occurred there. When we hear the word "circus," we think of three rings, clowns, and people on bicycles, but the circus in the Early New Testament was where all the chariot races occurred. It was a place where many Christians were killed for their faith, and many slaves were treated barbarically by others.

Christians believed they were dispatched into the world with a saving, healing, and redeeming message, and did not believe it was appropriate for them to sit and applaud when people were treated so horrifically. So they stayed away from the circus, and the world around them said, "What's wrong with these Christians? Can't they just *blend in* and be like the rest of us?"

Christians also declined participation in the theater because it was a place where deplorable things and depravity took place on the stage. If you think the movies today are disgraceful, know it is nothing new — it has always been that way, even in the First Century. Disgusting sexual things were carried out on the stage, and actors were called the lowest of the low because they were willing to do anything on the stage to get the applause of people.

The theater, actors, and actresses were associated with the god Dionysus, who was the god of drunkenness and orgies. All of that encompassed the theater scene. So Christians said, "We can't do that; we can't go and watch for entertainment. We need to stay away from that; we're redeemed."

Additionally, believers refused to attend athletic events because the athletes performed without clothing. Christians believed nudity was shameful, so they stayed away from the athletic events. Christians also stayed away from the bath houses because of the sexual acts that took place in them. So they said, "We can't go there and sit in the bath houses while all those things are going on around us."

Also, Christians were viewed generally as being unpatriotic which was a serious offense. First, they would not burn incense to the emperor, which meant they would not conform to the government's demands. Second, they wouldn't go into the temples because that's where sacrifices were being made to the gods. There was a lot of demonic activity and sexual situations in the temples, so Christians stayed away. The secular world thought, *What is wrong with these Christians? Why can't they just do what the government asks? Why can't they just blend in and be a little more like us?* So Christians were viewed as "Antipas" — *against everything*.

Israel Committed the Tragic Mistake of Moral Surrender

In Revelation 2:14, Jesus said, "But I have a few things against thee, because thou hast there them that hold the doctrine of Balaam, who taught Balac to cast a stumblingblock before the children of Israel, to eat things sacrificed unto idols, and to commit fornication."

The word "have" is the Greek word *echo*, which means *I have, I hold*, or *I possess*. It carries the idea of something Jesus feels deeply. The word "against" is the Greek word *kata*, which means I have *a strike against you*, and He tells us why. The word "hold" is the present active participle of the Greek word *kratos*, which depicts *a powerful grip*, and *refusal to let go*. It lets us know that Christ had already been dealing with this group telling them to let go of this wrong doctrine, but they wouldn't let it go. So Jesus basically said, "I have a few things against you. First, you are still holding onto the doctrine of Balaam."

Revelation 2:14 continues, "…The doctrine of Balaam, who taught Balac to cast a stumblingblock before the children of Israel, to eat things sacrificed unto idols, and to commit fornication." The word "stumblingblock," the Greek word *skandalon*, is where we get the word "scandal." It describes *a trap used to catch an animal*, and it carries the idea of *entrapment*. Balaam taught Balac how to entrap God's people — the children of Israel — into eating things that were sacrificed to idols.

In effect, Balaam said, "I don't have the power to curse the children of Israel. There are no enchantments, and there is no divination that can be used against them. So let's get the men of Israel to lower their bar morally; let's get them to make the tragic mistake of moral surrender. They'll do it by themselves, and it will cause divine judgment to fall."

Balaam instructed Balac to send naked Moabite women out in front of the children of Israel. Numbers 25:1-3 says, "And Israel abode in Shittim, and the people began to commit whoredom with the daughters of Moab. And they called the people unto the sacrifices of their gods: and the people did eat, and bowed down to their gods. And Israel joined himself unto Baalpeor: and the anger of the Lord was kindled against Israel."

Israel committed the tragic mistake of moral surrender. They joined themselves to Baalpeor, which means they *blended in*. Israel began to commit whoredom with the daughters of Moab. The men of Israel became so tolerant and compromised that they went to the place where sacrifices were being offered to the gods. The men ate what they should not have eaten. They bowed down to the gods, and accommodated what God despised. Israel morally surrendered, and the Lord's anger was kindled against them!

Hate Is a Strong Word, but Jesus Used It To Describe His Stance on What the Nicolaitanes Taught — Inclusivity and Tolerance

Revelation 2:15 says, "So hast thou also them that hold the doctrine of the Nicolaitanes, which thing I hate." The word "Nicolaitanes" is a translation of the Greek word *Nikolaos*, and it means *to conquer and subdue people* or *one who conquers and subdues people*.

What the Nicolaitans were teaching — *inclusivity and tolerance* — brought defeat to the people of God. In essence, God's people began to say, "Let's quit being so separate, and stop this. The world thinks of us as being antisocial. Let's quit talking about everything that is wrong, and just become more *inclusive* of everybody. Let's lower the bar and blend in so the people in the world won't think we're so antisocial."

Jesus said He *hates* this doctrine, and He *hated* the deeds of the Nicolaitanes. The word "hate" is the Greek word *miseo*, and means *to hate, to abhor*, or *to find utterly repulsive*. It pictures *a deep-seated animosity; intense hatred; repugnance;* or *something that causes one to feel disgust and repulsion*. It denotes *a deep-seated aversion; not just dislike, but actual hatred*. Jesus did not say he hated the Nicolaitans — He doesn't hate anybody, and we're not to hate anybody — but He hated their *deeds,* and He hated their *doctrine.*

Faulty beliefs result in a powerless, weakened version of Christianity where sin is tolerated, separation is ignored, and the need for ongoing repentance is disregarded. It pulls the plug on the power of the Gospel!

In Revelation we learn from Jesus Himself, there is a level of inclusivity and tolerance that He finds to be utterly disgusting. And my friend, when we feel a *pull* — from our family, our friends, and our kids — to accommodate everything that is around us, we need to remember the words of Jesus to the church of Pergamum: *We are to be uncompromising when it comes to absolute truth.*

STUDY QUESTIONS

> **Study to shew thyself approved unto God, a workman that needeth not to be ashamed, rightly dividing the word of truth.**
> **— 2 Timothy 2:15**

1. Psalm 119:101 says "I have refrained my feet from every evil way, that I might keep thy Word." When it comes to obeying the Word and abstaining from partaking of the evil of this world, what is your part? (Consider also Psalm 119:102-104.)

2. When the world tries to eliminate or "cancel" you because you won't comply to their ways of inclusivity and tolerance, realize you are godly and experiencing persecution (*see* 2 Timothy 3:12). What does the Bible tell us about persecution? (Consider Matthew 5:10-12; Second Corinthians 4:9; Romans 8:35-37; and Second Timothy 3:10-11.)

PRACTICAL APPLICATION

> **But be ye doers of the word, and not hearers only, deceiving your own selves.**
> **— James 1:22**

1. Antipas was a man who would not lower the bar nor violate his convictions. He was uncompromising when it came to his faith and what he believed. How about you? How far are you willing to go to stand up for the truth? When faced with peer pressure to conform to live like the world in the areas of tolerance and inclusivity, how do you respond? (*See* Romans 12:1,2.)

2. Notice the progression of Israel's moral surrender found in Numbers 25:1-3:
   - The men of Israel *lowered their standards* (when called unto the sacrifices of Baalpeor).
   - They *entertained* what was wrong (by eating what they shouldn't eat).
   - They *accommodated* what God despised (by bowing down to other gods).

The result? The anger of the Lord was kindled against them. What can you do to protect yourself from accommodating what God despises? Ask the Holy Spirit to help you do that.

LESSON 4

TOPIC
Moral Surrender for Society's Acceptance

SCRIPTURES
1. **Revelation 2:18** — ...These things saith the Son of God, who hath his eyes like unto a flame of fire, and his feet are like fine brass.
2. **Revelation 2:19** — I know thy works, and charity, and service, and faith, and thy patience, and thy works; and the last to be more than the first.
3. **Revelation 2:20** — Notwithstanding I have a few things against thee, because thou sufferest that woman Jezebel, which calleth herself a prophetess, to teach and to seduce my servants to commit fornication, and to eat things sacrificed unto idols.
4. **Revelation 2:21** — And I gave her space to repent of her fornication; and she repented not.
5. **Revelation 2:22** — Behold, I will cast her into a bed, and them that commit adultery with her into great tribulation, except they repent of their deeds.

GREEK WORDS

1. "flame of fire" — φλόγα πυρός (*phloga puros*): a blazing fire; a brightly burning fire with flames that are swirling, whirling, bending, twisting, turning and arching upward toward the sky
2. "fine brass" — χαλκολίβανον (*chalkolibanon*): a compound of the word *chalkos*, meaning brass or bronze, and the word *libanos*, meaning frankincense
3. "notwithstanding" — Ἀλλὰ (*alla*): indicates a pause; nonetheless; regardless; but even in spite of all this
4. "I have" — ἔχω (*echo*): to hold; to embrace; or to hold something very personally
5. "against" — κατά (*kata*): against; down; or a strike against someone; a forceful word that implies Christ would resist them until they repented of their deeds; carries a strong sense of domination and subjugation
6. "because" — ὅτι (*hoti*): indicates expressly the reason or purpose
7. "sufferest" — ἀφίημι (*aphiemi*): to permit, to release, to let go, to liberate, or to give unrestrained freedom
8. "calleth" — λέγουσα (*legousa*): alleging or asserting
9. "seduce" — πλανάω (*planao*): a moral wandering; pictures a person or nation who has veered from a solid path; as a result of veering morally, that person or nation is adrift; the word is the same word used to depict a lost animal that cannot find its way back home
10. "to commit fornication" — πορνεύω (*porneuo*): any type of sex with another person outside the bond of marriage; illicit sexual activity, including both adultery and homosexuality
11. "I gave" — ἔδωκα (*edoka*): I have given, indicating He had been dealing with her for a period of time
12. "space" — χρόνος (*chronos*): time; a season; a specified duration of time
13. "except" — ἐὰν (*ean*): shows the warning is conditional; in other words, the consequences may or may not happen, depending on how the hearer responds

SYNOPSIS

The emphasis of this lesson:

In order for the Christians of Thyatira to have jobs, they were required to be part of a trade guild and participate in pagan practices, drunken orgies, and debaucheries of all kinds. As Christians, we are not to accommodate the world's pressure to compromise for gain or in order to gain society's acceptance. Instead, we must remain uncompromising to the truth, and God will take care of us!

In our previous lesson, we learned about Christ's message to Pergamum. We saw that if you don't *agree* with society, it will do its best to "cancel" you. While they're calling for *us* to be tolerant and inclusive, the fact is, those who don't like what we believe are not very tolerant of us, and they certainly are not inclusive of us. They want to cancel us, but regardless of what the world does around us, we're called to stay on track and to be uncompromising in what we believe about what the Bible teaches.

Thyatira

Jesus also sent a message to Thyatira — a church that also had compromised and morally surrendered. The city of Thyatira was a military base positioned to prevent people from attacking the city of Pergamum. Pergamum was a treasure city filled with gold, statues, and art and it needed protection, so the city of Thyatira was established to its east to fulfill this role.

Because Thyatira was such a huge military base, all kinds of industries developed there. It had a thriving commercial center, which catered to sustaining the needs of the military. It had clothing businesses, animal caretakers, eating establishments, and defense-related industries. With all the commerce in the city of Thyatira, it became known for its famous trade guilds, which today we call "workers unions" or "trade unions."

The Trade Unions in Thyatira

It seems that Thyatira had the most sophisticated system of trade guilds anywhere in the entire Roman Empire. If a person was a member of a trade guild — or union — he was virtually guaranteed a job. But if he was not a member of a trade guild, he couldn't even *get* a job. This dominating influence in Thyatira became a challenge for Christians.

The trade guilds were filled with dark, pagan practices. For example, at the opening of their meeting, members were required to get on their knees and worship the patron god of that particular guild or union. Not only that, but there were drunken orgies, debaucheries of all kinds, and every member of the trade guild was expected to participate.

Christians in Thyatira were faced with a very difficult decision: Compromise their beliefs in order to remain in the trade guilds to be able to keep their jobs and earn a living — or honor God with their lives by opting out of the trade guilds because they simply could not compromise.

For Christians to remain a member of the trade guilds, they would have to make the tragic mistake of moral surrender. Those who didn't participate in debaucheries of all kinds either had their membership revoked, or they were blacklisted from getting a job in any other part of the city; they were essentially "canceled."

The Son of God's Eyes Were 'Like Unto a Flame of Fire' And Fire Brings Either Purification or Destruction

Jesus said, "And unto the angel of the church in Thyatira write; These things saith the Son of God, who hath his eyes like unto a flame of fire, and his feet are like fine brass" (Revelation 2:18). The words *phloga puros* — translated here as "flame of fire" — describes *a blazing fire, a brightly burning fire with flames that are swirling, whirling, bending, twisting, turning and arching upward toward the sky.*

In Scripture, fire was used either to purify or to destroy. The fact that Jesus was coming to this church with *fire* in His eyes indicates He first was coming to purify. However, if they refused to cooperate with the purification process, that same fire would bring judgment upon them.

Revelation 2:18 concludes, "…and his feet are like fine brass." When you read this in Greek it's perplexing because the words translated "fine brass" is the Greek word *chalkolibanon*, a compound of the word *chalkos*, meaning *brass or bronze*, and the word *libanos*, meaning *frankincense*. In this particular Greek word, bronze or brass and frankincense are pictured as alloys attempting to be mixed together. We know in the natural they could never be alloys, yet Jesus' feet are likened to "fine brass," a mixture of brass, bronze, *and* frankincense. What does that mean?

In Scripture, brass or bronze always represents *judgment*. Jesus was coming with feet of judgment. And frankincense, the very kind of frankincense used in the temple, represents high priestly intercessory *prayer*. Jesus' feet were drenched in frankincense — or high priestly intercessory prayer. While Christ's feet were prepared to move toward judgment if required, they were also saturated in intercessory prayer so that repentance would occur, and judgment would not need to take place.

Jesus Is Not in a Rush To Judge

Sometimes Christians are in a rush to judge, but Jesus is not in a hurry to judge. Addressing the church at Thyatira, His eyes deeply examined the situation. He came with eyes of fire to purify what was going on inside the church, but the same fire that could purify could also bring judgment. His feet were prepared to come in judgment, but *He was not in a rush to judge*. His feet were immersed in intercessory prayer so the church would hear His message and *self-correct* so judgment would not be needed.

The Bible says His feet were made of brass. In the program, Rick shared about a statue he keeps on the table in their TV room. He said, "…It is very, very heavy to pick up, because it is made of brass. It is *solid* brass. It is a big Russian bear, and the reason that I have it on my table is because many believe that the Russian bear is the symbol of Russia."

"And often when Denise and I are sitting watching something on television, she'll say, 'Rick, would you please move that bear so it doesn't obstruct my view.' Well, that's *quite* a request because it is very, very heavy! And every time Denise asks me to move it, I always think, *You don't understand what you're asking of me. This is really, really heavy!*"

Imagine what it would be like if you were walking with feet made out of brass. You wouldn't move very fast. You would lift each foot *very* slowly and proceed one step at a time. You couldn't run because your feet would be so heavy. And in Revelation 2:18, we find Jesus was not running to judgment. He was not rushing in judgment to the church of Thyatira who He had commanded to *repent*.

He gave them space to repent before judging them. And because His feet are drenched in *libanos* — frankincense, intercessory, high priestly prayer — we know that Jesus was praying that they would respond and self-correct before He ever got there. Friend, Jesus always gives you space to repent, and He doesn't rush into judgment.

Jesus Had a Few Things Against the Church of Thyatira That Called for Repentance

In some respects, the church of Thyatira was wonderful. Jesus said, "I know thy works, and charity, and service, and faith, and thy patience, and thy works; and the last to be more than the first" (Revelation 2:19). When you read this in Greek, it says, "I know the works *of you*, I know the charity *of you*, I know the service *of you*, the faith *of you*, the patience *of you*, and the works *of you*." This church was amazing when it came to walking in love.

Jesus confirmed His observation of His church in Thyatira saying, "I know uniquely the love, service, faith, and patience *of you*." He praised the believers for their charity, and He applauded them for their service. He commended them for their faith, and He celebrated them for their patience.

All of these were good things, but then He said, "Notwithstanding I have a few things against thee, because thou sufferest that woman Jezebel, which calleth herself a prophetess, to teach and to seduce my servants to commit fornication, and to eat things sacrificed unto idols" (Revelation 2:20).

The word "notwithstanding" is the Greek word *alla*, which indicates *a pause* or *a break in the text*. It means *nonetheless*; *regardless*; *but even in spite of all this*. Paraphrased, "notwithstanding" means, "Let's take a pause and transition to something that I need to deal with. In spite of all the amazing things you've done and are doing, I have a few things against you that I will forcibly take under control if needed."

Revelation 2:20 continues, "Notwithstanding I have…." The words "I have" are a form of the Greek word *echo*, which means *to hold*; *to embrace*; or *to hold something very personally*. It means that what Jesus saw in the church there, He felt it very *personally*. In essence, He said, "I have this, I hold this, and I really feel this."

He said, "I have a few things against thee." The word "against" is the Greek word *kata*, which means *against*; *down*; or *a strike against someone*. It is a forceful word that implies Christ would *resist them* until they repented of their deeds, and it carries a strong sense of *domination* and *subjugation*. It is the equivalent of saying, "As I've said, this is a strike against you that is personally disturbing Me. And if you don't deal with it correctly, I will take matters into My own hands and *I* will bring it under control." Wow!

What Was the Strike 'Against' the Church?

"Notwithstanding I have a few things against thee, because thou sufferest that woman Jezebel, which calleth herself a prophetess, to teach and to seduce my servants to commit fornication, and to eat things sacrificed unto idols" (Revelation 2:20). The word "because" is the Greek word *hoti*, and it indicates *expressly the reason or purpose*. In other words, Jesus said, "I'm going to tell you exactly why I'm upset and I'm going to be clear about it. It's because 'thou sufferest that woman Jezebel, which calleth herself a prophetess, to teach and to seduce my servants to commit fornication, and to eat things sacrificed to idols.'"

The word "sufferest" is a form of the Greek word *aphiemi*, which means *to permit, to release, to let go, to liberate*, or *to give unrestrained freedom*. It was the equivalent of Jesus saying, "No one has restrained or controlled this woman named Jezebel. She's been given free rein in the church to say and to do whatever she pleases."

The woman, Jezebel, first "calleth herself a prophetess." The word "calleth" us the Greek word *legousa*, which means *alleging* or *asserting*. It doesn't mean she *was* a prophetess, it was just what she is saying, or *asserting* about herself. She claimed to be a revelator with insight from God. And in the name of God she chose to "…teach and seduce my servants to commit fornication, and to eat things sacrificed unto idols" (Revelation 2:20).

The word "seduce" gives us insight into what Jezebel was teaching. It is the Greek word *planao*, and describes *a moral wandering*. It pictures *a person or nation who has veered from a solid path*, and *as a result of veering morally, that person or nation is adrift*. The word *planao* is the same word used to depict *a lost animal that cannot find its way back home*.

To be clear, the problem was not that *a woman* was teaching. Women can teach and preach! The problem was Jezebel was *seducing* and *abusing the position* that had been entrusted to her.

Jezebel Grieved the Spirit of God

Jezebel lowered the bar morally and taught Christ's servants not to be so strict morally. For the people of Thyatira, to keep their job they had to participate in trade guild activities, which included worshiping false gods, drunkenness, orgies, and all kinds of debaucheries. And for Christians to remain members of the trade guild and be accepted by society, they had to participate. If they withdrew from the trade guild, then they would lose their jobs and their income.

Jezebel basically taught, "It's okay to lower your standards. You don't have to live such a restricted separate lifestyle. Relax, and learn to be more inclusive and accommodating of other people's practices. You'll blend in and gain more acceptance by people in the world."

Compromising and lowering our standards pulls the plug on the power of God. Jezebel grieved the Spirit of God because she taught people to make the tragic mistake of moral surrender for the sake of society's acceptance. But God gave her time to repent.

God Gave Jezebel Space To Repent

How did Jezebel respond to God's grace and His correction? "And I gave her space to repent of her fornication, and she repented not" (Revelation 2:21). The words "I gave" are a form of the word *give* which means, *I have been giving*. Jesus had been dealing with Jezebel for a period of time, but she had not responded. The word "space" is the Greek word *chronos, and* it describes *time*; *a season*; or *a specified duration of time*. It is the equivalent of Jesus saying, "I have been giving her time to get this right. I've been giving her space to repent of her fornication."

Jezebel told believers to lower the standard, lower the bar, and blend in. She taught compromise, and Revelation 2:21 says, "...She repented not." The Greek literally says, "She did not *will* to repent of her fornication." She knew that Christ was calling upon her to repent, but she did not *will* to repent.

"Behold, I will cast her into a bed, and them that commit adultery with her into great tribulation..." (Revelation 2:22). This is a strong warning to Christian leaders who teach compromise or accommodation. The reproof continues, "...Except they repent of their deeds." The word "except" is amazing. It is the Greek word *ean*, and it shows *the warning is conditional*. In other words, *the consequences may or may not happen, depending on how the hearer responds*.

Remember, Jesus is not in a rush to judge. His feet are drenched in *libanos*, high priestly intercessory prayer. Jesus prays people will repent before He ever executes judgment. He gives us space to repent. But we need to remain uncompromising to the Bible, and *God will take care of us*.

Do you know someone who has wandered from the truth? In our next lesson, you'll discover what you can do to help them get back on track.

STUDY QUESTIONS

> Study to shew thyself approved unto God, a workman that needeth not to be ashamed, rightly dividing the word of truth.
> —2 Timothy 2:15

1. There is a right and a wrong use of authority. Jezebel used her position in a way that grieved the Spirit of God and caused God's servants to commit the tragic mistake of moral surrender. According to Ezekiel 34:1-10, what does the Bible say about using a leadership position in the church in a way that harms others?
2. What was God's response (*see* Ezekiel 34:11-16)?
3. "Take heed therefore unto yourselves, and to all the flock, over the which the Holy Ghost hath made you overseers, to feed the church of God, which he hath purchased with his own blood" (Acts 20:28). According to this verse, why are church leaders to take heed unto themselves? (Consider also James 3:1 and First Timothy 3:2-7.)
4. According to Revelation 2:20-22, what was Jesus' response to Jezebel's decision to teach and seduce God's servants to commit fornication, and eat things sacrificed to idols?

PRACTICAL APPLICATION

> But be ye doers of the word, and not hearers only, deceiving your own selves.
> —James 1:22

1. Take an honest, objective look at your life. Have you accommodated the ungodly ways of our society rather than living an uncompromising, holy life in line with God's Word? Like the church of Thyatira, are you doing great in some areas, yet tolerating sin in other areas? Take time now to repent of any compromise in your life and ask the Holy Spirit to purify you.
2. If you were faced with the situation where you had to compromise your standards to keep your job, or live by your convictions and be forced to quit your job as a result — what would you choose? Is God

big enough to provide a place for you to work that doesn't require you to compromise morally? (Consider Philippians 4:19.)

3. What is it that Jesus expects us to do when He comes with correction? How does He often send that correction? Are you willing to receive it? Consider Hebrews 12:5-11 and Second Timothy 3:16. Ask the Holy Spirit to help you receive any admonitions He has for you.

LESSON 5

TOPIC
God's Promise to People Who Help Wandering Saints Get Back on Track

SCRIPTURES
1. **James 5:19** — Brethren, if any of you do err from the truth, and one convert him;
2. **James 5:20** — Let him know, that he which converteth the sinner from the error of his way shall save a soul from death, and shall hide a multitude of sins.

GREEK WORDS
1. "brethren" — ἀδελφός (*adelphos*): a term used to describe two or more who were born from the same womb; later used in a military sense to depict brothers in battle; a comrade; hence, brotherhood
2. "if" — ἐάν (*ean*): the idea of a certain possibility; in all likelihood, it probably will happen
3. "any of you" — τις ἐν ὑμῖν (*tis en humin*): anyone in your midst
4. "err" — πλανάω (*planao*): a moral wandering; depicts a person who has veered from a solid path; as a result of veering morally, they are adrift; used to depict a lost animal that cannot find its path; to morally lose one's bearings
5. "from" — ἀπό (*apo*): away from; implies putting distance between oneself and something else

6. "the truth" — τῆς ἀληθείας (*tes aletheias*): a definite article with ἀλήθεια (*aletheia*); THE truth as revealed in Scripture
7. "convert" — ἐπιστρέφω (*epistrepho*): a turning point; to turn around; to turn back; to return
8. "know" — γινώσκω (*ginosko*): realize; fully comprehend
9. "converteth" — ἐπιστρέφω (*epistrepho*): a turning point; to turn around; to turn back; to return
10. "sinner" — ἁμαρτωλός (*hamartolos*): one who misses the mark and falls short of what God expects and approves
11. "from" — ἐκ (*ek*): out of
12. "error" — πλανάω (*planao*): a moral wandering; depicts one who has veered from a solid path; as a result of veering morally, he is adrift; depicts a lost animal that cannot find its path; to morally lose one's bearings
13. "way" — ὁδός (*hodos*): way; roads upon which one travels
14. "save" — σῴζω (*sodzo*): to heal, but also conveys the idea of wholeness or salvation; delivering and healing power that results in wholeness; to deliver from enemies; to protect, keep safe, to keep under protection
15. "from death" — ἐκ θανάτου (*ek thanatou*): from death; θάνατος (*thanatos*); can be physical or spiritual death, mortal danger, or a dangerous circumstance; a death sentence
16. "hide" — καλύπτω (*kalupto*): conceal; cover; veil; hide from view
17. "multitude of sins" — πλῆθος ἁμαρτιῶν (*plethos harmartion*): picturing fullness of sins

SYNOPSIS

The emphasis of this lesson:

When someone leaves the absolute authority of Scripture, this person has lost his or her anchor and is morally adrift. If you pray for someone who has wandered from the Truth and help them return to God, He promises, "…that he who turns a sinner from the error of his way will save a soul from death and cover a multitude of sins" (James 5:20 NKJV).

When you see people you love surrender morally, it breaks your heart. In fact, you wonder how they can believe what they're saying, and do what they're doing. How can they embrace what they are embracing when they were raised in the ways of God? The pressure of social media, education, the courts, Hollywood, or their environment influenced their compromise, and now they are morally adrift.

In Second Timothy 3, the apostle Paul prophesied under the anointing of the Holy Spirit that at the end of the age some people would sail into morally turbulent waters. The Holy Spirit told us this in advance, not to *scare* us, but to *prepare* us. The good news is that God can use you to make a difference in the lives of those who have gone morally adrift!

A Review of Our Previous Lessons on the Tragic Mistake of Moral Surrender

In our first lesson, we saw that Adam made the tragic mistake of moral surrender when he reached out willingly and partook of the forbidden fruit. With full understanding of what he was doing, Adam followed his wife, yielded to the temptation, and ate the fruit. And God held him accountable.

We need to be very careful as parents, grandparents, and friends that we don't succumb to what others are doing if they are veering morally. Don't be afraid and think, *If I don't accommodate them, or agree with them, I'm going to lose them.* My friend, that is not true. Your kids, your grandkids, and your friends need you to stay anchored in truth because one of these days when they're in trouble and need help, they're going to come looking for you. If you follow them by compromising your beliefs, you will not be in a position to help them. Stay on track and be uncompromising with the Word of God, even if your loved ones compromise.

Then we saw that Lot made the tragic mistake of moral surrender for opportunity. He was mesmerized by what the cities of Sodom and Gomorrah offered. For the sake of opportunity he accommodated a sinful environment, endorsed it, and even became a leader in the city of Sodom.

Lot blended into his wicked surroundings, and completely compromised himself. As a result, he lost everything. He lost his wife, and his daughters got into sin. He should have stayed on track and chosen to not compromise on what he knew to be true. But God delivered Lot because Abraham prayed for his nephew — and He will deliver those you're concerned about when you pray for them!

Next, we saw the story of the Nicolaitans who made the tragic mistake of moral surrender by embracing inclusivity and tolerance. There is pressure today for us to include *everybody* and to be tolerant of *everything*. Certainly, we need to be kind, but in Revelation 2, Jesus calls us to be uncompromising to the Word of God.

And we learned the church of Thyatira made the tragic mistake of moral surrender for society's acceptance. As Christians, we are not to accommodate the world's pressure to compromise in order to gain society's acceptance. Instead, we must remain uncompromising to the truth, and God will take care of us! My friend, we need to live according to what God commands us in His Word.

You Can Help Saints Who Have Morally Wandered Get Back on Track

Moral wandering was occurring back when James wrote his epistle, and it continues to happen today. But there is something you can do to help. James 5:19 and 20 says, "Brethren, if any of you do err from the truth, and one convert him; Let him know, that he which converteth the sinner from the error of his way shall save a soul from death, and shall hide a multitude of sins."

Even as early as when James was writing this epistle, believers were already beginning to stray from their faith. People were heartbroken because they saw their loved ones or their friends veer from what they knew to be right in spite of the fact they once embraced the truth. And that is what's happening today.

Because of social media, the courts, education, movies, and more, young people are growing up with pressures that other generations didn't experience to this degree. They are bombarded from every direction and are pressured to either *abandon* their faith or *modify* it. People are endorsing things that are not in line with the Bible, including all kinds of strange sexual beliefs. It's nonsense, but if you are unwavering in your stance for the truth, society says you should be "canceled."

Knowing the believers needed direction in this area, James said, "Brethren, if any of you do err from the truth, and one convert him…" (James 5:19). The word "brethren" is the Greek word *adelphos*. It is a term used to describe *two or more who were born from the same womb*. Later, this term *adelphos* — translated "brethren" — was used in a military sense to depict *brothers in battle*; *a comrade*; and hence, *brotherhood*. It describes two or more people who are endearing to each other. It's such an appropriate word to portray all of us because we are all mutually born out of the womb of God. We've been born again, born of God, and therefore we are related.

James spoke to people dealing with all kinds of fights and struggles, and he called them "brethren." It's the equivalent of saying, "I know you're in the trenches, and I know you're dealing with issues, but *my comrades*, I have something to say to you." Then he adds, "…If any of you do err from the truth…" (James 5:19). The word "if" in Greek is the word *ean*, and carries the idea *of a certain possibility*. It means *in all likelihood*; *it probably will happen*. Somewhere along the way, each one of us will know someone who errs from the truth, and we need to know how to deal with it.

When Someone Veers Morally They Become Morally Adrift

The phrase, "if any of you" is translated from the Greek words *tis en humin* and means *anyone in your midst*. Our head needs to be up, and our eyes need to be open to be watchful for anyone near us who does "err from the truth" (James 5:19). The word "err" is a form of the Greek word *planao*, and it is used throughout the New Testament.

The word "err" is a very specific word that describes *a moral wandering*. It denotes *a person who has veered from a solid path* or *to morally lose one's bearings*. It depicts *a lost animal that cannot find its path*. Notice, this doesn't just describe error, but *a moral wandering*. It pictures a person who has turned away from a solid path that he once walked on. As a result of veering morally, this individual is now morally *adrift*.

When people leave the absolute authority of Scripture and no longer receive it as God's voice to them, they are morally *adrift*. They've lost their anchor, and there is no end to where they may go because they've left the authoritative voice of the Scripture. Like an animal that gets so lost it can't find the path to get back home again, when someone becomes morally adrift, they have lost their moral bearings and have lost sight of the correct path.

Because of the onslaught of information being promoted and endorsed — through social media, what the courts are passing down by law, and the crazy things that are being taught in schools — kids today are confused. Some boys don't know that they're boys, and some girls don't know that they're girls. They think maybe they can become something they were not born to be. We're living in a day where *society* has lost its moral anchor and is *adrift*.

In James 5:19, James added, "...if any of you do err *from* the truth...." The word "from" is an important word because it is translated from the Greek word *apo*, and it means *away from*. It implies *putting distance between oneself and something else*. When people begin to err, morally wander, and become morally adrift, they begin to put space between themselves and others because they know many loved ones don't agree with what they're doing. They put distance between themselves and the Bible, or gaps between themselves and the church. They put space between themselves and what they used to be and become *distant*.

James 5:19 continues, "...if any of you do err from the truth, and one convert him." In Greek, the word "truth" has a definite article, which means this is THE *truth as revealed in Scripture*. When someone has wandered from the truth, it is a departure from the authoritative voice of the Word of God. People become adrift because they severed their vital connection to *the truth* contained in Scripture. The word "convert" is the Greek word *epistrepho*, and it describes *a turning point*. It means *to turn around* or *to turn back*. Here, it denotes *to return* to what once was or to what one once believed.

There Is Hope for Those Who Have Missed the Mark

James continued, "Let him *know*, that he which converteth the sinner from the error of his way shall save a soul from death, and shall hide a multitude of sins" (James 5:20). Let *who* know? James is addressing the person who is willing to go after the one who has morally wandered. The word "know" is a form of the Greek word *ginosko*, and it means to *realize* or *fully comprehend*. God wants you to *fully know* something, and it's found in the next part of the verse.

"Let him know, that he which *converteth* the *sinner* from the error of his way...." "Converteth," again, the Greek word *epistrepho*, depicts *a turning point*, *to turn around* or *to turn back*. It carries the idea of someone *returning* to what he or she once believed and *being* who he or she once was. How powerful and encouraging! And the word "sinner" is a translation of the Greek word *hamartolos*, meaning *one who misses the mark and falls short of what God expects and approves*. Literally, we can help someone who has missed the mark to turn around and find their way back.

The word "from" here is a translation of the Greek word *ek*, which means *out of*, and carries the idea of deliverance. "Error," again, the Greek word *planao*, depicts *a moral wandering* or *a loss of one's bearings*. It pictures one who is *adrift and has veered from a solid path*. And the word "way" is the Greek word *hodos*, which means *a road that one travels upon*. The Bible tells us where this error-filled road is headed unless the person is converted and returns to Christ. If we avail ourselves to God, we can be used as instruments of deliverance. We can be used by God to deliver those who have lost their bearings from the error of their ways.

Saving a Soul From Death and Hiding a Multitude of Sins

What is the result of getting a wandering soul back on track? James 5:20 says when you convert someone who has veered off the road he was travelling on and is adrift, you will "save [his] soul from death." Wow! The word "save" is a form of the Greek word *sodzo*, and it means *to heal*, but it also conveys the idea of *wholeness or salvation*. It is a *delivering and healing power that results in wholeness*. The word *sodzo* — "save" — denotes *to deliver from enemies, to protect, to keep safe*, and *to keep under protection* even if someone is in the enemy's clutches. There is healing and delivering power available for *anyone*, regardless of how far they have veered morally. They can be delivered and brought back under the protective care of God.

James said you will save a soul "from death." The phrase "from death" is a translation of the Greek words *ek thanatou*. The word *ek* means *out of*, and the word *thanatos* depicts *physical or spiritual death*, but it also carries the idea of *mortal danger*, or *a dangerous circumstance or situation*. This tells us when someone veers morally, they're headed down a road that is carrying them to mortal danger. They are in a dangerous situation that they can be delivered out of.

Furthermore, James 5:20 says, "…And shall hide a multitude of sins." God is in the business of *forgiving* and *covering* sins with the blood of Jesus. The word "hide" is the Greek word *kalupto*, and means *to conceal; cover; veil*; or *hide from view*. James 5:20 goes on to say he shall hide a "multitude of sins," translated from the Greek words *plethos harmartion*. This pictures a *fullness of sins* and carries the idea of being filled to the maximum and overflowing. There is no limit on the amount of sin that the blood of Jesus will cover.

God's Healing and Delivering Power Are Available to Everyone!

If a person gets off track and drifts, and their life is overflowing with a multitude of sins, they experience tragic consequences. If they don't repent, if they don't convert and get back on track, they are headed for mortal danger. But God wants to use *you* to intervene.

Abraham stood before the Lord on Lot's behalf, and when God was about to destroy Sodom and Gomorrah, the Lord rescued Lot because He remembered Abraham's intercession (*see* Genesis 19:29). Just as Abraham interceded for Lot, you can draw near to the Lord and pray for those who have morally wandered. God will save, deliver, heal, rescue, restore, and bring them back under His divine protection. His grace and mercy will cover it all. That's God's promise to you for anyone you are concerned about!

Friend, we do not need to be in a rush to judge anybody. We certainly don't want to condemn people we love. We need to understand if they've missed the mark and fallen short of what God expects and approves, it's time to help them *return* to the truth of God's Word and get back on track again. The reward is life-changing and eternal.

STUDY QUESTIONS

Study to shew thyself approved unto God, a workman that needeth not to be ashamed, rightly dividing the word of truth.
— 2 Timothy 2:15

1. In Second Samuel 12:1-13, Nathan the prophet was sent to deliver a message to David, the King of Israel, who had erred from *the truth* by committing adultery, and then having a man killed. Can you imagine the level of intimidation in approaching the king? Nathan was given a riveting message and delivered it in the fear of the Lord. It was so well received that the first words out of King David's mouth after hearing the message were, "I have sinned against the Lord" (2 Samuel 12:13). How did God use Nathan to reach David and bring him to the point

of repentance? Are you willing to be used to help others come back to Jesus?

2. Look at the raw response of David when Nathan delivered the word of the Lord as seen in Psalm 51:1-13,17. He cried out for mercy, acknowledged his sin, and returned to "...truth in the inward parts..." (Psalm 51:6). In response to David's genuine repentance from erring from *the truth*, God honored David's prayer, "...Create in me a clean heart, O God; and renew a right spirit within me..." (Psalm 51:10). What is your response when the Lord convicts you of sin?

3. Just as Nathan the prophet was sent by the Lord to minister to David, God can use you to speak a word in season to those who are adrift (*see* Isaiah 50:4). First Corinthians 14:1 (*ESV*) instructs us to earnestly desire spiritual gifts. Ask God for the gifts of the Spirit to operate through you and realize that flowing in the gifts can help a sinner repent and return from his moral wandering (*see* First Peter 4:10). May you "...Come behind in no gift; waiting for the coming of our Lord..." (1 Corinthians 1:7).

PRACTICAL APPLICATION

> But be ye doers of the word, and not hearers only,
> deceiving your own selves.
> —James 1:22

"My brothers, if anyone among you wanders from the truth and someone brings him back, let him know that whoever brings back a sinner from his wandering will save his soul from death and will cover a multitude of sins" (James 5:19,20 *ESV*).

Do you know and love someone who has morally wandered away from the truth? Here are some practical ways to apply the vital truths of this lesson:

1. **Pray in tongues.** The Holy Spirit will pray out the strategies needed to reach the person who has gone adrift. He knows what lured them into moral wandering, and how to rescue them out of it. As you pray in tongues, the Holy Spirit will, "...Maketh intercession for the saints according to the will of God" (Romans 8:27). Pray much in tongues over the situation.

2. **Listen to the Holy Spirit.** As you pray for the person who has morally wandered, over time keep your spiritual ears open for direction

from the Holy Spirit regarding anything you need to do in addition to praying for the individual.
3. **Obey the Holy Spirit's leading.** "…Whatever He says, do it" (John 2:5 *AMPC*). Realize that *when* is just as important as *what*, so follow Him in the timing of your bold obedience.
4. **Stay in faith.** Don't waiver in your faith. By faith, see the person walking with God again even if it takes more time for their deliverance than you expected. They have a will, and they need to make a quality decision to return to Christ. According to Hebrews 6:12, through faith and patience you obtain the promise, so don't "…Grow weary of doing good, for in due season we will reap, if we do not give up" (Galatians 6:9 *ESV*). (Consider also Luke 15:11-24; Romans 4:17-21; and Hebrews 10:35.)

Notes

Notes

Notes

CLAIM YOUR FREE RESOURCE!

As a way of introducing you further to the teaching ministry of Rick Renner, we would like to send you free of charge his teaching CD, "How To Receive a Miraculous Touch From God."

In His earthly ministry, Jesus commonly healed *all* who were sick of *all* their diseases. In this profound message, learn about the manifold dimensions of Christ's wisdom, goodness, power, and love toward all humanity who came to Him in faith with their needs.

☑ **YES, I want to receive Rick Renner's monthly teaching letter!**

Simply scan the QR code to claim this resource or go to:
renner.org/claim-your-free-offer

WITH US!

renner.org   facebook.com/rickrenner
youtube.com/rennerministries   instagram.com/rickrrenner

www.ingramcontent.com/pod-product-compliance
Lightning Source LLC
Chambersburg PA
CBHW061257040426
42444CB00010B/2405